⌐S⌐LAUREATE SERIES

ALTO SAXOPHONE MUSIC

TUNING
Before the piano accompaniment begins you will hear four tuning notes, followed by a short scale and another tuning note. This will enable you to tune your instrument to the record.

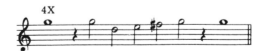

MMO CD 4112
Cass. No. 8022

COMPACT DISC PAGE AND BAND INFORMATION

MMO CD 4112
MMO Cass. 8022

LAUREATE SERIES CONTEST SOLOS
BEGINNING LEVEL FOR ALTO SAX, VOL. 2

<table>
<tr><td>Band No.
Complete
Version</td><td></td><td>Band No.
Minus
Alto Sax</td><td>Page
No.</td></tr>
<tr><td>1</td><td>***Mozart:*** Minuet</td><td>9</td><td>6</td></tr>
<tr><td>2</td><td>***Borodin:*** Polovtsian Dance</td><td>10</td><td>7</td></tr>
<tr><td>3</td><td>***Tenaglia:*** Aria Antica</td><td>11</td><td>8</td></tr>
<tr><td>4</td><td>***Rameau:*** La Vilageoise</td><td>12</td><td>9</td></tr>
<tr><td></td><td>La Vilageoise (Slow Version)</td><td>13</td><td>9</td></tr>
<tr><td>5</td><td>***Ravel:*** Pavane Pour Une Infante Defunte</td><td>14</td><td>10</td></tr>
<tr><td>6</td><td>***Young:***</td><td></td><td></td></tr>
<tr><td></td><td>Contempora Suite, III Saraband</td><td>15</td><td>11</td></tr>
<tr><td>7</td><td>IV Gigue</td><td>16</td><td>12</td></tr>
<tr><td></td><td>IV Gigue (Slow Version)</td><td>17</td><td>12</td></tr>
<tr><td>8</td><td>Piano Tuning Notes</td><td></td><td></td></tr>
</table>

PERFORMANCE GUIDE
COMMENTARY BY VINCENT ABATO

MOZART
Minuet from *Haffner Music, K. 250*

The accents are very important. Start the trill above the note.

There should be no change of tempo. Exaggerate the *sforzando* in the beginning.

BORODIN
Polovtsian Dance from *Prince Igor*

Every time you have an ornament use the C key plus the left hand D sharp (which is the top key on the instrument) with your left index finger. The tonality is not the most important thing. Rather, you should strive for clarity. The grace notes are not accented.

TENAGLIA
Aria Antica

In the third measure from the end, start the trill with the regular C sharp to D fingering to establish the tonality of the note. Then, as you increase the speed of the trill, go to the top D sharp key. Because this is an easier fingering, you will be able to trill faster. The speed of the trill is even more important than the quality of the note.

RAMEAU
La Villageoise

Play very smoothly and stately. Don't rush the sixteenth notes beginning in measure 33. Watch the dynamic markings in order to get contrast.

RAVEL
Pavane pour une Infante Defunte

We made a ritard at the end but played *a tempo* where marked (6 before the end). Observe the dynamics. Keep the volume down.

MMO CD 4112
Cass. No. 8022

YOUNG
Sarabande and Gigue from *The Contempora Suite*

We did the *Sarabande* in a slow four. Notice the phrasing of the eighth note groups in the first, third, seventh bars, etc.

In the *Gigue,* the pick-up notes should be exactly in rhythm. It may be a good idea for the student to count, so that the eighth notes leading into the downbeat will not be too late. The accents are very important. This piece fits the style of the baroque period.

MINUET
from "Haffner Music," K.250

WOLFGANG A. MOZART
Trans. By Himie Voxman

♩ = 126 (4'02")

5 beats precede music

Allegro moderato

POLOVTSIAN DANCE
from "Prince Igor"

ALEXANDER BORODIN
Arr. By Harold L. Walters

ARIA ANTICA

♩ = 80 (3' 15")

ANTONIO TENAGLIA
Arr. By Quinto Maganini

MMO CD 4112
Cass. No. 8022

LA VILLAGEOISE

♩ = 84 (1'48")
♩ = 69 (2'10")

JEAN P. RAMEAU
Arr. By A. Louis Scarmolin

4 beats precede music

PAVANE POUR UNE INFANTE DEFUNTE

MAURICE RAVEL
Arr. By Harold L. Walters

MMO CD 4112
Cass. No. 8022

CONTEMPORA SUITE
Third Movement: Saraband

GORDON YOUNG

MMO CD 4112
Cass. No. 8022

Fourth Movement: Gigue

MUSIC MINUS ONE ALTO SAXOPHONE

ALTO SAXOPHONE (Eb Instrument)

ALTO SAXOPHONE SOLOS Student Edition **Volume 1** .... **MMO CD 4101**
Adios Muchachos; After The Ball; Ah, So Pure; American Patrol; America; Battle Hymn; The Band Played On; Beautiful Isle; Because; Daisy Bell; Eli, Eli; El Chocio; Fantasie Impromptu; Finlandia; Fur Elise; Glow Worm; Gypsy Love; Hatikvoh; Holy City; I Love You Truly; I'll Sing Thee; Songs Of Araby; In Old Madrid; Just A-Wearyin' For You; Kathleen Mavourneen; Kentucky Babe; La Cumparsita; La Paloma; La Spagnola; March Slav; Mexican Hat Dance; Might Lak' A Rose; Oh Promise Me; O Sole Mio!; Pomp And Circumstance; Red River Valley; The Rosary; Santa Lucia; Serenade **V. Herbert;** Song of India; Sweet Rosy O'Grady; **Rachmaninoff** Piano Concerto; **MacDowell** To A Wild Rose; Vilia; Who is Sylvia?

ALTO SAXOPHONE SOLOS Student Edition **Volume 2**... **MMO CD 4102**
Ain't Gonna Study War No More; Berceuse; Black Is The Color; Bluebeard; Blues in Eb; Careless Love **J.S. Bach:** Chorale No.83; Cradle Song; Far Above Cayuga's Waters; Fireball Polka; Greensleeves; Hello Ma Baby; High School Cadets; H.M.S. Pinafore; In Dulci Jubilo **J.S. Bach:** Jesu, Joy Of Man's Desiring; Little Brown Jug; **Sousa:** Manhattan Beach **Borodin:** Melody **Prince Igor** (Moderato); Mr. Frog Went A Courtin'!; Nocturne; Old Paint; On Top of Old Smoky; Peter and the Wolf; Recruiting Song **Sousa:** Rifle Regiment; **Rimsky Korsakoff** Scheherazade; The Sidewalks of New York; Spanish Guitar **Sousa:** Stars & Stripes; The Cossack; Theme from Moldau; **Bizet:** Toreador Song; Valse Noble; When I Was Single; When The Saints Go Marchin' In; You Tell Me Your Dreams; Young Prince & Princess.

EASY JAZZ DUETS FOR ALTO SAXOPHONE .... **MMO CD 4103**
Easy to medium duets performed by Hal McKusick, Alto Sax Star, and YOU! Graded for the lst, 2nd, 3rd and 4th year student, these duets are a joy to hear and play. You're accompanied by the Benny Goodman rhythm section, laying down a bed of easy to follow rhythm tracks. The rhythm section, George Duvivier and Bobby Donaldson, jazz legends.

FOR SAXES ONLY .... **MMO CD 4104**
Join an All-Star Band as lead Alto or Tenor in arrangements styled after the Basie and Ellington Bands. Tailored for your horn, this album includes Bb and Eb parts plus suggested improvisations. A totally unique experience in playing with a professional sax section, and an absolute must for stage band players. *Conceived and Arranged by Bob Wilber*

TEACHER'S PARTNER Basic Alto Sax Studies 1st year .... **MMO CD 4105**
Tune to C; Play from C to G; Solo in C; G Scales; Solo in G; Duet in G; F Scales ; Solo in F; Duet in F; D Scales; Solo in D; Duet in D; Bb Scales; Solo in Bb; Duet in Bb; C Scales; Solo in C; Duet in C; Scale Cycle; G Scale; Solo in Bb; Graduation Piece.

BEGINNING CONTEST SOLOS .... **MMO CD 4111**
J.S. Bach: Gavotte **Bizet:** Intermezzo **Chopin:** Largo **Dvorak:** Larghetto **Gretchaninoff:** Evening Waltz **Grieg:** Album Leaf **Haydn:** Andante **Kreisler:** Rondino **Mozart:** Ave Verum **Weber:** Hunter's Chorus. *Paul Brodie, Canadian Soloist*

BEGINNING CONTEST SOLOS .... **MMO CD 4112**
Borodin: Polovtsian Dance **Mozart:** Minuet **Rameau:** La Villageoise **Ravel:** Pavane **Tenaglia:** Aria Antica **Young:** Contempora Suite (3rd & 4th mvts.) *Vincent Abato, Metropolitan Opera Orch.*

INTERMEDIATE CONTEST SOLOS .... **MMO CD 4113**
J.S. Bach: Andante Cantabile **Beethoven:** Romance **Bizet:** Minuet **Blavet:** Adagio and Gigue **Handel:** Bouree
Paul Brodie, Canadian Soloist

INTERMEDIATE CONTEST SOLOS .... **MMO CD 4114**
J.S. Bach: Air **D'Ambrosio:** Canzonetta **Français:** Cinq Danses Exotiques (Mambo. Samba et Merengue) **Mozart:** Sonatina **Mussorgsky:** The Old Castle **Platti:** Sonata No. 5 (3rd mvt.) *Vincent Abato, Metropolitan Opera Orchestra*

ADVANCED CONTEST SOLOS .... **MMO CD 4115**
Benson: Farewell **Jacob:** Rhapsody **Vivaldi:** Concerto in A Minor (3rd mvt.) **Whitney:** Rhumba.
Paul Brodie, Canadian Soloist

ADVANCED CONTEST SOLOS .... **MMO CD 4116**
Creston: Sonata (2nd & 3rd mvts.) **Rabaud:** Solo de Concours **Schubert:** The Bee *Vincent Abato, Metropolitan Opera Orchestra*

ADVANCED CONTEST SOLOS .... **MMO CD 4117**
Jacob: Sonata 1st mvt. **Vivaldi:** Sonata in G Minor **Ward:** An Abstract *Paul Brodie, Canadian Soloist*

ADVANCED CONTEST SOLOS .... **MMO CD 4118**
Eccles: Sonata (lst. 2nd & 4th mvts.) **Gurewich:** Concerto (3rd mvt.) **Handel:** Adagio and Allegro **Heiden:** Sonata (2nd mvt.)
Vincent Abato, Metropolitan Opera Orchestra

BLUES FUSION Arranged by Eric Kriss .... **MMO CD 4205**
Tricky Dicky; When The Spirit; Cocaine Stomp; Wailer Blues; Boogie Breakdown; Tremblin'; Yancey's Fancy; Mad Dog Blues.

JOBIM'S BOSSA NOVA'S .... **MMO CD 4206**
The Girl From Ipanema; So Danço Samba; Once I Loved; Dindi; One Note Samba; Meditation
How Insensitive; Triste; Quiet Nights Of Quiet Stars (Corcovado); Wave *John Sergenian, Solist*
Indulge yourself in these lush and lovely orchestral backgrounds minus Alto or Tenor Sax.
Listen to a 'pro' play them, then 'reed-up' and become a 'latin bird' surrounded by gorgeous string arrangements.

EVOLUTION OF THE BLUES Clark Terry/Bob Wilber .... **MMO CD 7004**
Blues in all styles and time signatures. Listen to melody line then improvisation followed by jamming space *for you*. Indispensable!

THE ART OF IMPROVISATION, VOL. 1 .... **MMO CD 7005**
Rich Matteson & Jack Petersen's Course on Jazz Improvisation, Developed at N. Texas State Univ. the seed-bed for the stage band movement in America. C, Bb, Eb, Bass Clef parts supplied.

THE ART OF IMPROVISATION, VOL. 2 .... **MMO CD 7006**

TEN BLUES MINUS YOU For All Instrumentalists Arranged by Mal Waldron. .... **MMO CD 7007**
Mal Waldron's classic study of various blues stylings, performed by Ed Xiques multi-instrumentalist, and by you.

TAKE A CHORUS Solos & Arrangements by Jimmy Raney. .... **MMO CD 7008**
How About You; Beta Minus; Darn That Dream; This Heart Of Mine; Fools Rush In; Spring Is Here; Sunday; I Got It Bad; Just You, Just Me; Jupiter. *Ed Xiques, Soloist*

All MMO's are complete with printed music for the omitted part.

MUSIC MINUS ONE TENOR SAXOPHONE

TENOR SAX (Bb Instrument)

ALTO SAXOPHONE SOLOS Student Edition Volume 1 .... **MMO CD 4101**
Adios Muchachos; After The Ball; Ah, So Pure; American Patrol; America; Battle Hymn; The Band Played On; Beautiful Isle; Because; Daisy Bell; Eli, Eli; El Chocio; Fantasie Impromptu; Finlandia; Fur Elise; Glow Worm; Gypsy Love; Hatikvoh; Holy City; I Love You Truly; I'll Sing Thee; Songs Of Araby; In Old Madrid; Just A-Wearyin' For You; Kathleen Mavourneen; Kentucky Babe; La Cumparsita; La Paloma; La Spagnola; March Slav; Mexican Hat Dance; Might Lak' A Rose; Oh Promise Me; O Sole Mio!; Pomp And Circumstance; Red River Valley; The Rosary; Santa Lucia; Serenade **V. Herbert**; Song of India; Sweet Rosy O'Grady; **Rachmaninoff** Piano Concerto; **MacDowell** To A Wild Rose; Vilia; Who is Sylvia?

ALTO SAXOPHONE SOLOS Student Edition Volume 2 .... **MMO CD 4102**
Ain't Gonna Study War No More; Berceuse; Black Is The Color; Bluebeard; Blues in Eb; Careless Love **J.S. Bach**: Chorale No.83; Cradle Song; Far Above Cayuga's Waters; Fireball Polka; Greensleeves; Hello Ma Baby; High School Cadets; H.M.S. Pinafore; In Dulci Jubilo **J.S. Bach**: Jesu, Joy Of Man's Desiring; **Sousa**: Manhattan Beach **Borodin**: Melody **Prince Igor** (Moderato); Mr. Frog Went A Courtin'!; Nocturne; Old Paint; On Top of Old Smoky; Peter and the Wolf; Recruiting Song **Sousa**: Rifle Regiment; **Rimsky Korsakoff** Scheherazade; The Sidewalks of New York; Spanish Guitar **Sousa**: Stars & Stripes; The Cossack; Theme from Moldau; **Bizet**: Toreador Song; Valse Noble; When I Was Single; When The Saints Go Marchin' In; You Tell Me Your Dreams; Young Prince & Princess.

EASY JAZZ DUETS with Rhythm Section .... **MMO CD 4203**
Duets from the easiest 1st year level up thru difficult material that would challenge the 2nd, 3rd and 4th year player. Play with jazz icon Zoot Sims, George Duvivier on bass and Bobby Donaldson on drums. These duets will also delight the professional, in their simplicity of execution.

FOR SAXES ONLY .... **MMO CD 4204**
Join an All-Star Band as lead Alto or Tenor in arrangements styled after the Basie and Ellington Bands. Tailored for Alto or Tenor, this album includes Bb and Eb parts plus suggested improvisations. A unique experience in playing with professional sax section, An absolute *must* for stage band players. *Conceived and Arranged by Bob Wilber*

BLUES FUSION Arranged by Eric Kriss .... **MMO CD 4205**
Tricky Dicky; When The Spirit; Cocaine Stomp; Wailer Blues; Boogie Breakdown; Tremblin'; Yancey's Fancy; Mad Dog Blues

JOBIM'S BOSSA NOVA'S .... **MMO CD 4206**
The Girl From Ipanema; So Danço Samba; Once I Loved; Dindi; One Note Samba; Meditation
How Insensitive; Triste; Quiet Nights Of Quiet Stars (Corcovado); Wave   *John Sergenian, Soloist*
Indulge yourself in these lush and lovely orchestral backgrounds minus Alto or Tenor Sax.
Listen to a 'pro' play them, then 'reed-up' and become a 'latin bird' surrounded by gorgeous string arrangements.

EVOLUTION OF THE BLUES Clark Terry/Bob Wilber .... **MMO CD 7004**
Blues in all styles and time signatures. Listen to melody line then improvisation followed by jamming space *for you*. Indispensable!

THE ART OF IMPROVISATION, VOL. 1 .... **MMO CD 7005**
Rich Matteson & Jack Petersen's Course on Jazz Improvisation, Developed at N. Texas State Univ. The seed-bed for the stage band movement in America. C, Bb, Eb, Bass Clef parts supplied.

THE ART OF IMPROVISATION, VOL. 2 .... **MMO CD 7006**

TEN BLUES MINUS YOU For All Instrumentalists Arranged by Mal Waldron. .... **MMO CD 7007**
Mal Waldron's classic study of various blues stylings, performed by Ed Xiques multi-instrumentalist, and by you.

TAKE A CHORUS Solos & Arrangements by Jimmy Raney. .... **MMO CD 7008**
How About You; Beta Minus; Darn That Dream; This Heart Of Mine; Fools Rush In; Spring Is Here; Sunday; I Got It Bad; Just You, Just Me; Jupiter.   *Ed Xiques, Soloist*

All MMO's are complete with printed music for the omitted part.

MMO Compact Disc Catalog

BROADWAY

LES MISERABLES/PHANTOM OF THE OPERA	MMO CD 1016
HITS OF ANDREW LLOYD WEBBER	MMO CD 1054
GUYS AND DOLLS	MMO CD 1067
WEST SIDE STORY 2 CD Set	MMO CD 1100
CABARET 2 CD Set	MMO CD 1110
BROADWAY HEROES AND HEROINES	MMO CD 1121
CAMELOT	MMO CD 1173
BEST OF ANDREW LLOYD WEBBER	MMO CD 1130
THE SOUND OF BROADWAY	MMO CD 1133
BROADWAY MELODIES	MMO CD 1134
BARBRA'S BROADWAY	MMO CD 1144
JEKYLL & HYDE	MMO CD 1151
SHOWBOAT	MMO CD 1160
MY FAIR LADY 2 CD Set	MMO CD 1174
OKLAHOMA!	MMO CD 1175
THE SOUND OF MUSIC 2 CD Set	MMO CD 1176
SOUTH PACIFIC	MMO CD 1177
THE KING AND I	MMO CD 1178
FIDDLER ON THE ROOF 2 CD Set	MMO CD 1179
CAROUSEL	MMO CD 1180
PORGY AND BESS	MMO CD 1181
THE MUSIC MAN	MMO CD 1183
ANNIE GET YOUR GUN 2 CD Set	MMO CD 1186
HELLO DOLLY! 2 CD Set	MMO CD 1187
OLIVER 2 CD Set	MMO CD 1189
SUNSET BOULEVARD	MMO CD 1193
GREASE	MMO CD 1196
SMOKEY JOE'S CAFE	MMO CD 1197
MISS SAIGON	MMO CD 1226

CLARINET

MOZART CONCERTO, IN A	MMO CD 3201
WEBER CONCERTO NO. 1 in Fm. STAMITZ CONC. No. 3 IN Bb	MMO CD 3202
SPOHR CONCERTO NO. 1 in C MINOR OP. 26	MMO CD 3203
WEBER CONCERTO OP. 26, BEETHOVEN TRIO OP. 11	MMO CD 3204
FIRST CHAIR CLARINET SOLOS	MMO CD 3205
THE ART OF THE SOLO CLARINET:	MMO CD 3206
MOZART QUINTET IN A, K.581	MMO CD 3207
BRAHMS SONATAS OP. 120 NO. 1 & 2	MMO CD 3208
WEBER GRAND DUO CONCERTANT WAGNER ADAGIO	MMO CD 3209
SCHUMANN FANTASY OP. 73, 3 ROMANCES OP. 94	MMO CD 3210
EASY CLARINET SOLOS Volume 1 - STUDENT LEVEL	MMO CD 3211
EASY CLARINET SOLOS Volume 2 - STUDENT LEVEL	MMO CD 3212
EASY JAZZ DUETS - STUDENT LEVEL	MMO CD 3213
BEGINNING CONTEST SOLOS - Jerome Bunke, Clinician	MMO CD 3221
BEGINNING CONTEST SOLOS - Harold Wright	MMO CD 3222
INTERMEDIATE CONTEST SOLOS - Stanley Drucker	MMO CD 3223
INTERMEDIATE CONTEST SOLOS - Jerome Bunke, Clinician	MMO CD 3224
ADVANCED CONTEST SOLOS - Stanley Drucker	MMO CD 3225
ADVANCED CONTEST SOLOS - Harold Wright	MMO CD 3226
INTERMEDIATE CONTEST SOLOS - Stanley Drucker	MMO CD 3227
ADVANCED CONTEST SOLOS - Stanley Drucker	MMO CD 3228
ADVANCED CONTEST SOLOS - Harold Wright	MMO CD 3229
BRAHMS Clarinet Quintet in Am, Op. 115	MMO CD 3230
TEACHER'S PARTNER Basic Clarinet Studies	MMO CD 3231
JEWELS FOR WOODWIND QUINTET	MMO CD 3232
WOODWIND QUINTETS minus CLARINET	MMO CD 3233

PIANO

BEETHOVEN CONCERTO NO 1 IN C	MMO CD 3001
BEETHOVEN CONCERTO NO. 2 IN Bb	MMO CD 3002
BEETHOVEN CONCERTO NO. 3 IN C MINOR	MMO CD 3003
BEETHOVEN CONCERTO NO. 4 IN G	MMO CD 3004
BEETHOVEN CONCERTO NO. 5 IN Eb (2 CD SET)	MMO CD 3005
GRIEG CONCERTO IN A MINOR OP.16	MMO CD 3006
RACHMANINOFF CONCERTO NO. 2 IN C MINOR	MMO CD 3007
SCHUMANN CONCERTO IN A MINOR	MMO CD 3008
BRAHMS CONCERTO NO. 1 IN D MINOR (2 CD SET)	MMO CD 3009
CHOPIN CONCERTO NO. 1 IN E MINOR OP. 11	MMO CD 3010
MENDELSSOHN CONCERTO NO. 1 IN G MINOR	MMO CD 3011
MOZART CONCERTO NO. 9 IN Eb K.271	MMO CD 3012
MOZART CONCERTO NO. 12 IN A K.414	MMO CD 3013
MOZART CONCERTO NO. 20 IN D MINOR K.466	MMO CD 3014
MOZART CONCERTO NO. 23 IN A K.488	MMO CD 3015
MOZART CONCERTO NO. 24 IN C MINOR K.491	MMO CD 3016
MOZART CONCERTO NO. 26 IN D K.537, CORONATION	MMO CD 3017
MOZART CONCERTO NO. 17 IN G K.453	MMO CD 3018
LISZT CONCERTO NO. 1 IN Eb, WEBER OP. 79	MMO CD 3019
LISZT CONCERTO NO. 2 IN A, HUNGARIAN FANTASIA	MMO CD 3020
J.S. BACH CONCERTO IN F MINOR, J.C. BACH CON. IN Eb	MMO CD 3021
J.S. BACH CONCERTO IN D MINOR	MMO CD 3022
HAYDN CONCERTO IN D	MMO CD 3023
HEART OF THE PIANO CONCERTO	MMO CD 3024
THEMES FROM GREAT PIANO CONCERTI	MMO CD 3025
TSCHAIKOVSKY CONCERTO NO. 1 IN Bb MINOR	MMO CD 3026
ART OF POPULAR PIANO PLAYING, Vol. 1 STUDENT LEVEL	MMO CD 3033
ART OF POPULAR PIANO PLAYING, Vol. 2 STUDENT LEVEL 2 CD Set	MMO CD 3034
'POP' PIANO FOR STARTERS STUDENT LEVEL	MMO CD 3035
MOZART COMPLETE MUSIC FOR PIANO FOUR HANDS 2 CD Set	MMO CD 3036
DVORAK TRIO IN A MAJOR, OP. 90 "Dumky Trio"	MMO CD 3037
DVORAK QUINTET IN A MAJOR, OP. 81	MMO CD 3038
MENDELSSOHN TRIO IN D MAJOR, OP. 49	MMO CD 3039
MENDELSSOHN TRIO IN C MINOR, OP. 66	MMO CD 3040

PIANO - FOUR HANDS

RACHMANINOFF Six Scenes	4-5th year	MMO CD 3027
ARENSKY 6 Pieces, STRAVINSKY 3 Easy Dances	2-3rd year	MMO CD 3028
FAURE Dolly Suite	3-4th year	MMO CD 3029
DEBUSSY Petite Suite	3-4th year	MMO CD 3030
SCHUMANN Pictures from the East	4-5th year	MMO CD 3031
BEETHOVEN Three Marches	4-5th year	MMO CD 3032
MAYKAPAR First Steps, OP. 29	1-2nd year	MMO CD 3041
TSCHAIKOVSKY Fifty Russian Folk Songs	1-2nd year	MMO CD 3042

INSTRUCTIONAL METHODS

RUTGERS UNIVERSITY MUSIC DICTATION/EAR TRAINING COURSE (7 CD Set)	MMO CD 7001
EVOLUTION OF THE BLUES	MMO CD 7004
THE ART OF IMPROVISATION, VOL. 1	MMO CD 7005
THE ART OF IMPROVISATION, VOL. 2	MMO CD 7006
THE BLUES MINUS YOU Ed Xiques, Soloist	MMO CD 7007
TAKE A CHORUS minus Bb/Eb Instruments	MMO CD 7008

VIOLIN

BRUCH CONCERTO NO. 1 IN G MINOR OP.26	MMO CD 3100
MENDELSSOHN CONCERTO IN E MINOR	MMO CD 3101
TSCHAIKOVSKY CONCERTO IN D OP. 35	MMO CD 3102
BACH DOUBLE CONCERTO IN D MINOR	MMO CD 3103
BACH CONCERTO IN A MINOR, CONCERTO IN E	MMO CD 3104
BACH BRANDENBURG CONCERTI NOS. 4 & 5	MMO CD 3105
BACH BRANDENBURG CONCERTO NO. 2,TRIPLE CONCERTO	MMO CD 3106
BACH CONCERTO IN DM, (FROM CONCERTO FOR HARPSICHORD)	MMO CD 3107
BRAHMS CONCERTO IN D OP. 77	MMO CD 3108
CHAUSSON POEME, SCHUBERT RONDO	MMO CD 3109
LALO SYMPHONIE ESPAGNOLE	MMO CD 3110
MOZART CONCERTO IN D K.218, VIVALDI CON. AM OP.3 NO.6	MMO CD 3111
MOZART CONCERTO IN A K.219	MMO CD 3112
WIENIAWSKI CON. IN D. SARASATE ZIGEUNERWEISEN	MMO CD 3113
VIOTTI CONCERTO NO.22	MMO CD 3114
BEETHOVEN 2 ROMANCES, SONATA NO. 5 IN F "SPRING SONATA"	MMO CD 3115
SAINT-SAENS INTRODUCTION & RONDO, MOZART SERENADE K. 204, ADAGIO K.261	MMO CD 3116
BEETHOVEN CONCERTO IN D OP. 61(2 CD SET)	MMO CD 3117
THE CONCERTMASTER	MMO CD 3118
AIR ON A G STRING Favorite Encores with Orchestra Easy Medium	MMO CD 3119
CONCERT PIECES FOR THE SERIOUS VIOLINIST Easy Medium	MMO CD 3120
18TH CENTURY VIOLIN PIECES	MMO CD 3121
ORCHESTRAL FAVORITES - Volume 1 - Easy Level	MMO CD 3122
ORCHESTRAL FAVORITES - Volume 2 - Medium Level	MMO CD 3123
ORCHESTRAL FAVORITES - Volume 3 - Med to Difficult Level	MMO CD 3124
THE THREE B'S BACH/BEETHOVEN/BRAHMS	MMO CD 3125
VIVALDI Concerto in A Minor Op. 3 No. 6. in D Op. 3 No. 9. Double Concerto Op. 3 No. 8	MMO CD 3126
VIVALDI-THE FOUR SEASONS (2 CD Set)	MMO CD 3127
VIVALDI Concerto in Eb, Op. 8, No. 5. ALBINONI Concerto in A	MMO CD 3128
VIVALDI Concerto in E, Op. 3, No. 12. Concerto in C Op. 8, No. 6 "Il Piacere"	MMO CD 3129
SCHUBERT Three Sonatinas	MMO CD 3130
HAYDN String Quartet Op. 76 No. 1	MMO CD 3131
HAYDN String Quartet Op. 76 No. 2	MMO CD 3132
HAYDN String Quartet Op. 76 No. 3 "Emperor"	MMO CD 3133
HAYDN String Quartet Op. 76 No. 4 "Sunrise"	MMO CD 3134
HAYDN String Quartet Op. 76 No. 5	MMO CD 3135
HAYDN String Quartet Op. 76 No. 6	MMO CD 3136
BEAUTIFUL MUSIC FOR TWO VIOLINS 1st position, vol. 1	MMO CD 3137 ★
BEAUTIFUL MUSIC FOR TWO VIOLINS 2nd position, vol. 2	MMO CD 3138 ★
BEAUTIFUL MUSIC FOR TWO VIOLINS 3rd position, vol. 3	MMO CD 3139 ★
BEAUTIFUL MUSIC FOR TWO VIOLINS 1st, 2nd, 3rd position, vol. 4	MMO CD 3140 ★
BARTOK: 44 DUETS	MMO CD 3141
TEACHER'S PARTNER Basic Violin Studies 1st year	MMO CD 3142
DVORAK STRING TRIO "Terzetto", OP. 74 2 violins/viola	MMO CD 3143

★Lovely folk tunes and selections from the classics, chosen for their melodic beauty and technical value. They have been skillfully transcribed and edited by Samuel Applebaum, one of America's foremost teachers.

CELLO

DVORAK Concerto in B Minor Op. 104 (2 CD Set)	MMO CD 3701
C.P.E. BACH Concerto in A Minor	MMO CD 3702
BOCCHERINI Concerto in Bb, BRUCH Kol Nidrei	MMO CD 3703
TEN PIECES FOR CELLO	MMO CD 3704
SCHUMANN Concerto in Am & Other Selections	MMO CD 3705
CLAUDE BOLLING Suite For Cello & Jazz Piano Trio	MMO CD 3706

OBOE

ALBINONI Concerti in Bb, Op. 7 No. 3, No. 6, Dm Op. 9 No. 2	MMO CD 3400
TELEMANN Conc. in Fm; HANDEL Conc. in Bb; VIVALDI Conc.in Dm	MMO CD 3401
MOZART Quartet in F K.370, STAMITZ Quartet in F Op. 8 No. 3	MMO CD 3402
BACH Brandenburg Concerto No. 2, Telemann Con. in Am	MMO CD 3403
CLASSIC SOLOS FOR OBOE Delia Montenegro, Soloist	MMO CD 3404
MASTERPIECES FOR WOODWIND QUINTET	MMO CD 3405
WOODWIND QUINTETS minus OBOE	MMO CD 3406

GUITAR

BOCCHERINI Quintet No. 4 in D "Fandango"	MMO CD 3601
GIULIANI Quintet in A Op. 65	MMO CD 3602
CLASSICAL GUITAR DUETS	MMO CD 3603
RENAISSANCE & BAROQUE GUITAR DUETS	MMO CD 3604
CLASSICAL & ROMANTIC GUITAR DUETS	MMO CD 3605
GUITAR AND FLUTE DUETS Volume 1	MMO CD 3606
GUITAR AND FLUTE DUETS Volume 2	MMO CD 3607
BLUEGRASS GUITAR CLASSIC PIECES minus you	MMO CD 3608
GEORGE BARNES GUITAR METHOD Lessons from a Master	MMO CD 3609
HOW TO PLAY FOLK GUITAR 2 CD Set	MMO CD 3610
FAVORITE FOLKS SONGS FOR GUITAR	MMO CD 3611
FOR GUITARS ONLY! Jimmy Raney Small Band Arrangements	MMO CD 3612
TEN DUETS FOR TWO GUITARS Geo. Barnes/Carl Kress	MMO CD 3613
PLAY THE BLUES GUITAR A Dick Weissman Method	MMO CD 3614
ORCHESTRAL GEMS FOR CLASSICAL GUITAR	MMO CD 3615

BANJO

BLUEGRASS BANJO Classic & Favorite Banjo Pieces	MMO CD 4401
PLAY THE FIVE STRING BANJO Vol. 1 Dick Weissman Method	MMO CD 4402
PLAY THE FIVE STRING BANJO Vol. 2 Dick Weissman Method	MMO CD 4403

FLUTE

MOZART Concerto No. 2 in D, QUANTZ Concerto in G	MMO CD 3300
MOZART Concerto in G K.313	MMO CD 3301
BACH Suite No. /2 in B Minor	MMO CD 3302
BOCCHERINI Concerto in D, VIVALDI Concerto in G Minor "La Notte", MOZART Andante for Strings	MMO CD 3303
HAYDN Divertimento, VIVALDI Concerto in D Op. 10 No. 3 "Bullfinch", FREDERICK THE GREAT Concerto in C	MMO CD 3304
VIVALDI Conc. in F; TELEMANN Conc. in D; LECLAIR Conc. in C	MMO CD 3305
BACH Brandenburg No. 2 in F, HAYDN Concerto in D	MMO CD 3306
BACH Triple Concerto, VIVALDI Concerto in D Minor	MMO CD 3307
MOZART Quartet in F, STAMITZ Quartet in F	MMO CD 3308
HAYDN 4 London Trios for 2 Flutes & Cello	MMO CD 3309
BACH Brandenburg Concerti Nos. 4 & 5	MMO CD 3310
MOZART 3 Flute Quartets in D, A and C	MMO CD 3311
TELEMANN Suite in A Minor, GLUCK Scene from 'Orpheus', PERGOLESI Concerto in G 2 CD Set	MMO CD 3312
FLUTE SONG: Easy Familiar Classics	MMO CD 3313
VIVALDI Concerti In D, G, and F	MMO CD 3314
VIVALDI Concerti in A Minor, G. and D	MMO CD 3315
EASY FLUTE SOLOS Beginning Students Volume 1	MMO CD 3316
EASY FLUTE SOLOS Beginning Students Volume 2	MMO CD 3317
EASY JAZZ DUETS Student Level	MMO CD 3318
FLUTE & GUITAR DUETS Volume 1	MMO CD 3319
FLUTE & GUITAR DUETS Volume 2	MMO CD 3320
BEGINNING CONTEST SOLOS Murray Panitz	MMO CD 3321
BEGINNING CONTEST SOLOS Donald Peck	MMO CD 3322
INTERMEDIATE CONTEST SOLOS Julius Baker	MMO CD 3323
INTERMEDIATE CONTEST SOLOS Donald Peck	MMO CD 3324
ADVANCED CONTEST SOLOS Murray Panitz	MMO CD 3325
ADVANCED CONTEST SOLOS Julius Baker	MMO CD 3326
INTERMEDIATE CONTEST SOLOS Donald Peck	MMO CD 3327
ADVANCED CONTEST SOLOS Murray Panitz	MMO CD 3328
INTERMEDIATE CONTEST SOLOS Julius Baker	MMO CD 3329
BEGINNING CONTEST SOLOS Doriot Anthony Dwyer	MMO CD 3330
INTERMEDIATE CONTEST SOLOS Doriot Anthony Dwyer	MMO CD 3331
ADVANCED CONTEST SOLOS Doriot Anthony Dwyer	MMO CD 3332
FIRST CHAIR SOLOS with Orchestral Accompaniment	MMO CD 3333
TEACHER'S PARTNER Basic Flute Studies 1st year	MMO CD 3334
THE JOY OF WOODWIND MUSIC	MMO CD 3335
WOODWIND QUINTETS minus FLUTE	MMO CD 3336

RECORDER

PLAYING THE RECORDER Folk Songs of Many Naitons	MMO CD 3337
LET'S PLAY THE RECORDER Beginning Children's Method	MMO CD 3338
YOU CAN PLAY THE RECORDER Beginning Adult Method	MMO CD 3339

FRENCH HORN

MOZART Concerti No. 2 & No. 3 in Eb. K. 417 & 447	MMO CD 3501
BAROQUE BRASS AND BEYOND	MMO CD 3502
MUSIC FOR BRASS ENSEMBLE	MMO CD 3503
MOZART Sonatas for Two Horns	MMO CD 3504
BEGINNING CONTEST SOLOS Mason Jones	MMO CD 3511
BEGINNING CONTEST SOLOS Myron Bloom	MMO CD 3512
INTERMEDIATE CONTEST SOLOS Dale Clevenger	MMO CD 3513
INTERMEDIATE CONTEST SOLOS Mason Jones	MMO CD 3514
ADVANCED CONTEST SOLOS Myron Bloom ,	MMO CD 3515
ADVANCED CONTEST SOLOS Dale Clevenger	MMO CD 3516
INTERMEDIATE CONTEST SOLOS Mason Jones	MMO CD 3517
ADVANCED CONTEST SOLOS Myron Bloom	MMO CD 3518
INTERMEDIATE CONTEST SOLOS Dale Clevenger	MMO CD 3519
FRENCH HORN WOODWIND MUSIC	MMO CD 3520
WOODWIND QUINTETS minus FRENCH HORN	MMO CD 3521

TRUMPET

THREE CONCERTI: HAYDN, TELEMANN, FASCH	MMO CD 3801
TRUMPET SOLOS Student Level Volume 1	MMO CD 3802
TRUMPET SOLOS Student Level Volume 2	MMO CD 3803
EASY JAZZ DUETS Student Level	MMO CD 3804
MUSIC FOR BRASS ENSEMBLE Brass Quintets	MMO CD 3805
FIRST CHAIR TRUMPET SOLOS with Orchestral Accompaniment	MMO CD 3806
THE ART OF THE SOLO TRUMPET with Orchestral Accompaniment	MMO CD 3807
BAROQUE BRASS AND BEYOND Brass Quintets	MMO CD 3808
THE COMPLETE ARBAN DUETS all of the classic studies	MMO CD 3809
SOUSA MARCHES PLUS BEETHOVEN, BERLIOZ, STRAUSS	MMO CD 3810
BEGINNING CONTEST SOLOS Gerard Schwarz	MMO CD 3811
BEGINNING CONTEST SOLOS Armando Ghitalla	MMO CD 3812
INTERMEDIATE CONTEST SOLOS Robert Nagel, Soloist	MMO CD 3813
INTERMEDIATE CONTEST SOLOS Gerard Schwarz	MMO CD 3814
ADVANCED CONTEST SOLOS Robert Nagel, Soloist	MMO CD 3815
ADVANCED CONTEST SOLOS Armando Ghitalla	MMO CD 3816
INTERMEDIATE CONTEST SOLOS Gerard Schwarz	MMO CD 3817
ADVANCED CONTEST SOLOS Robert Nagel, Soloist	MMO CD 3818
ADVANCED CONTEST SOLOS Armando Ghitalla	MMO CD 3819
BEGINNING CONTEST SOLOS Raymond Crisara	MMO CD 3820
BEGINNING CONTEST SOLOS Raymond Crisara	MMO CD 3821
INTERMEDIATE CONTEST SOLOS Raymond Crisara	MMO CD 3822
TEACHER'S PARTNER Basic Trumpet Studies 1st year	MMO CD 3823

TROMBONE

TROMBONE SOLOS Student Level Volume 1	MMO CD 3901
TROMBONE SOLOS Student Level Volume 2	MMO CD 3902
EASY JAZZ DUETS Student Level	MMO CD 3903
BAROQUE BRASS & BEYOND Brass Quintets	MMO CD 3904
MUSIC FOR BRASS ENSEMBLE Brass Quintets	MMO CD 3905
BEGINNING CONTEST SOLOS Per Brevig	MMO CD 3911
BEGINNING CONTEST SOLOS Jay Friedman	MMO CD 3912

INTERMEDIATE CONTEST SOLOS Keith Brown, Professor, Indiana University	MMO CD 3913
INTERMEDIATE CONTEST SOLOS Jay Friedman	MMO CD 3914
ADVANCED CONTEST SOLOS Keith Brown, Professor, Indiana University	MMO CD 3915
ADVANCED CONTEST SOLOS Per Brevig	MMO CD 3916
ADVANCED CONTEST SOLOS Keith Brown, Professor, Indiana University	MMO CD 3917
ADVANCED CONTEST SOLOS Jay Friedman	MMO CD 3918
ADVANCED CONTEST SOLOS Per Brevig	MMO CD 3919
TEACHER'S PARTNER Basic Trombone Studies 1st year	MMO CD 3920

DOUBLE BASS

BEGINNING TO INTERMEDIATE CONTEST SOLOS David Walter	MMO CD 4301
INTERMEDIATE TO ADVANCED CONTEST SOLOS David Walter	MMO CD 4302
FOR BASSISTS ONLY Ken Smith, Soloist	MMO CD 4303
THE BEAT GOES ON Jazz - Funk, Latin, Pop-Rock	MMO CD 4304

TENOR SAX

TENOR SAXOPHONE SOLOS Student Edition Volume 1	MMO CD 4201
TENOR SAXOPHONE SOLOS Student Edition Volume 2	MMO CD 4202
EASY JAZZ DUETS FOR TENOR SAXOPHONE	MMO CD 4203
FOR SAXES ONLY Arranged by Bob Wilber	MMO CD 4204

ALTO SAXOPHONE

ALTO SAXOPHONE SOLOS Student Edition Volume 1	MMO CD 4101
ALTO SAXOPHONE SOLOS Student Edition Volume 2.	MMO CD 4102
EASY JAZZ DUETS FOR ALTO SAXOPHONE	MMO CD 4103
FOR SAXES ONLY Arranged Bob Wilber	MMO CD 4104
BEGINNING CONTEST SOLOS Paul Brodie, Canadian Soloist	MMO CD 4111
BEGINNING CONTEST SOLOS Vincent Abato	MMO CD 4112
INTERMEDIATE CONTEST SOLOS Paul Brodie, Canadian Soloist	MMO CD 4113
INTERMEDIATE CONTEST SOLOS Vincent Abato	MMO CD 4114
ADVANCED CONTEST SOLOS Paul Brodie. Canadian Soloist	MMO CD 4115
ADVANCED CONTEST SOLOS Vincent Abato	MMO CD 4116
ADVANCED CONTEST SOLOS Paul Brodie, Canadian Soloist	MMO CD 4117
ADVANCED CONTEST SOLOS Vincent Abato	MMO CD 4118
TEACHER'S PARTNER Basic Alto Sax Studies 1st year	MMO CD 4119

DRUMS

MODERN JAZZ DRUMMING 2 CD Set	MMO CD 5001
FOR DRUMMERS ONLY	MMO CD 5002
WIPE OUT	MMO CD 5003
SIT-IN WITH JIM CHAPIN	MMO CD 5004
DRUM STAR Trios/Quartets/Quintets Minus You	MMO CD 5005
DRUMPADSTICKSKIN Jazz play-alongs with small groups	MMO CD 5006
CLASSICAL PERCUSSION 2 CD Set	MMO CD 5009
EIGHT MEN IN SEARCH OF A DRUMMER	MMO CD 5010

VOCAL

SCHUBERT GERMAN LIEDER - High Voice, Volume 1	MMO CD 4001
SCHUBERT GERMAN LIEDER - Low Voice, Volume 1	MMO CD 4002
SCHUBERT GERMAN LIEDER - High Voice, Volume 2	MMO CD 4003
SCHUBERT GERMAN LIEDER - Low Voice, Volume 2	MMO CD 4004
BRAHMS GERMAN LIEDER - High Voice	MMO CD 4005
BRAHMS GERMAN LIEDER - Low Voice	MMO CD 4006
EVERYBODY'S FAVORITE SONGS - High Voice, Volume 1	MMO CD 4007
EVERYBODY'S FAVORITE SONGS - Low Voice, Volume 1	MMO CD 4008
EVERYBODY'S FAVORITE SONGS - High Voice, Volume 2	MMO CD 4009
EVERYBODY'S FAVORITE SONGS - Low Voice, Volume 2	MMO CD 4010
17th/18th CENT. ITALIAN SONGS - High Voice, Volume 1	MMO CD 4011
17th/18th CENT. ITALIAN SONGS - Low Voice, Volume 1	MMO CD 4012
17th/18th CENT. ITALIAN SONGS - High Voice, Volume 2	MMO CD 4013
17th/18th CENT. ITALIAN SONGS - Low Voice, Volume 2	MMO CD 4014
FAMOUS SOPRANO ARIAS	MMO CD 4015
FAMOUS MEZZO-SOPRANO ARIAS	MMO CD 4016
FAMOUS TENOR ARIAS	MMO CD 4017
FAMOUS BARITONE ARIAS	MMO CD 4018
FAMOUS BASS ARIAS	MMO CD 4019
WOLF GERMAN LIEDER FOR HIGH VOICE	MMO CD 4020
WOLF GERMAN LIEDER FOR LOW VOICE	MMO CD 4021
STRAUSS GERMAN LIEDER FOR HIGH VOICE	MMO CD 4022
STRAUSS GERMAN LIEDER FOR LOW VOICE	MMO CD 4023
SCHUMANN GERMAN LIEDER FOR HIGH VOICE	MMO CD 4024
SCHUMANN GERMAN LIEDER FOR LOW VOICE	MMO CD 4025
MOZART ARIAS FOR SOPRANO	MMO CD 4026
VERDI ARIAS FOR SOPRANO	MMO CD 4027
ITALIAN ARIAS FOR SOPRANO	MMO CD 4028
FRENCH ARIAS FOR SOPRANO	MMO CD 4029
ORATORIO ARIAS FOR SOPRANO	MMO CD 4030
ORATORIO ARIAS FOR ALTO	MMO CD 4031
ORATORIO ARIAS FOR TENOR	MMO CD 4032
ORATORIO ARIAS FOR BASS	MMO CD 4033
BEGINNING SOPRANO SOLOS Kate Hurney	MMO CD 4041
INTERMEDIATE SOPRANO SOLOS Kate Hurney	MMO CD 4042
BEGINNING MEZZO SOPRANO SOLOS Fay Kittelson	MMO CD 4043
INTERMEDIATE MEZZO SOPRANO SOLOS Fay Kittelson	MMO CD 4044
ADVANCED MEZZO SOPRANO SOLOS Fay Kittelson	MMO CD 4045
BEGINNING CONTRALTO SOLOS Carline Ray	MMO CD 4046
BEGINNING TENOR SOLOS George Shirley	MMO CD 4047
INTERMEDIATE TENOR SOLOS George Shirley	MMO CD 4048
ADVANCED TENOR SOLOS George Shirley	MMO CD 4049

BASSOON

SOLOS FOR THE BASSOON Janet Grice, Soloist	MMO CD 4601
MASTERPIECES FOR WOODWIND MUSIC	MMO CD 4602
WOODWIND QUINTETS minus BASSOON	MMO CD 4603

VIOLA

VIOLA SOLOS with piano accompaniment	MMO CD 4501
DVORAK QUINTET IN A, Opus 81	MMO CD 4502
DVORAK STRING TRIO "Terzetto", OP. 74 2 Vins/Viola	MMO CD 4503

MMO MUSIC GROUP, INC., 50 Executive Boulevard, Elmsford, NY 10523-1325